LITTLE ROGER THE DODGER
AND HIS JOURNEY HOME...

It was a beautiful day in London and at the London Zoo, zookeeper officer Dibbs was doing his rounds. He first stopped at the koala bear cage where little Roger the Dodger was kept. Little Roger was sitting in a puddle of tears.

'Good morning, Roger. Why are you so upset?' zookeeper Dibbs asked.

'Well, Officer Dibbs, my parents' house is on fire and I'm terribly worried about them,' Roger the Dodger explained.

'Oh, that's right Roger. I heard the news regarding Kangaroo Island in South Australia. I am so very sorry, Roger.

'Do you know how it all started, Officer Dibbs?' Roger asked.

'Well, Roger, the news said there was a violent storm and dry brush struck by lightning started the fire.'

'A dry brush?' asked Roger. 'Why was it so dry?'
'Well, Roger, you see, the world we live in is becoming hotter and hotter each year because we don't take care of it as we should. There is an old saying, Roger. It's not how you start out doing things, it is how you finish them that counts. My very best wishes to you and your family, take care of yourself.'

Little Roger the Dodger noticed officer Dibbs forgot to lock his cage as he left. 'Dibbs! Dibbs! Where are you?' he shouted after him. 'You have forgotten to lock my cage!'

'Oh, my gosh!' little Roger the Dodger exclaimed. 'I cannot see him. Or anyone, for the matter. Hmm? I could escape and make a run for it and somehow try to get home to check on Mom and Dad. I hope I don't get caught.'

And then, little Roger the Dodger stepped out of his cage and tip-toed quietly past his neighbors, No one was in sight. 'Oh my' I can already see the exit sign. I'd better not try to go through there,' he muttered to himself and made a run toward the bushes.

Little Roger the Dodger reached the fence behind the bushes that surround the zoo and looked over the fence.
'So this is where all that noise and smell comes from!' he exclaimed. 'There are so many smelly cars out here!'

As little Roger the Dodger looked over the fence, he realized very quickly it was a long way down. It would be a whole lot easier if I had a parachute. 'I'm going down!' he shouted and in no time reached the pavement with a loud thump!

He started running at high speed.

I'm away.' I'm a fast runner. They won't catch me - that's why I'm called Little Roger the Dodger.'

He approached a garbage truck and overheard a conversation between the two trashmen. 'Hey, Ernie, put that trash can down, we have a full truck, mate. We need to empty it and we'll come back.'

'Ok, Burt.'

As the two men drove away, Little Roger thought, 'Golly, so much garbage!'

Roger walked past the trash cans which were left behind and noticed a bike that someone had thrown away. He looked at it and thought, 'Wow! Why would someone throw away a cool red bike rather than give it to someone who doesn't have one? Perhaps, I could ride it all the way home.

And there's also a blue jeans jacket and some goggles. Dress like that and nobody will notice me now.'

He grabbed the jacket and put it on. Then, he reached for the goggles.

'This is cool. I feel like a racer! I really like going fast, I feel the need for ....you know what I mean!'

As he was racing down the sidewalk, he did a sharp left turn and saw a sign on a wall which read Paddington. 'That name rings a bell. I must be close to The City of London,' he thought.

As he went down another sidewalk which was covered in trees, he thought: 'This is awesome, no one will spot me now.' And then something else caught his attention.

'Cool. This must be the River Thames. It's a giant river that connects to the ocean,' Roger thought to himself.

'And that must be the famous Tower Bridge!' he shouted excitedly. It's a terrific bridge and it's about 135 years old. I have read all about the City of London.' But then an awful thought occurred to him: 'Water? I didn't think about that! How will I get home? I can't ride my bike across the ocean
...hmm.'

A lady in a black car shouted at Roger: 'Hello, young man, that is a super red bicycle you have there.'

'Oh, hello! Thank you. How are you?' he asked politely, thinking, 'I hope she doesn't recognize me as the missing Koala from the zoo.'

Roger continued riding and a found park covered in trees. I need somewhere to hide, and this park is perfect. Nobody will be able to see me in these trees. In the meantime, I need to figure out how I'm going to get home.

In the center of the park, there was an opening with a massive pond. 'What an awesome pond. I'll see if I can make some friends.'

Roger pulled up to the water's edge and said: 'Hey, there! How are you guys?' '

We are terrific. My name is Goosey, and this is my friend lady Sig. What's your name?' 'My name is Roger.' 'Where are you going on your bike?' Goosey asked. 'That is a good question. I am going home to Australia to see my mom and dad but I can't ride home on a bike. I've been trying to decide how to get there instead.' 'I've been to Australia,' said Goosey. 'You have?' Roger asked amazed. 'Hmm, now that you mention it, I could take you.' 'Wow, really?' 'Yes. It's a long flight, about 12000 miles. We would have to fly north first, then south, all the way around the globe.'

'That is really kind of you, Goosey'.

Next to the pond, a little girl was playing soccer with her dad. Roger was super-duper impressed with her soccer skills. 'Is this how you do it, Dad?' the girl was asking her Dad as Roger walked up to him.

'Hello, my name is Little Roger the Dodger. I am going to give my bike away and I was wondering if your daughter would like to have it? 'Well, hello, Little Roger the Dodger,' said the Dad, turning to Roger. 'My name is David and I am sure, my daughter Ellie would love the bike!'

'Ellie, what do you think about the bike?' Roger asked.

'It's awesome and it is my favorite color, red. Thank you very much, Mr. Little Roger Dodger.'

'You're welcome, Ellie. It does go fast, so, please, be careful.

'Hop-on, Roger,' said Goosey. 'I don't need a runway. I've just got to clear those trees up ahead,' Roger nodded. 'This is your captain speaking. Thanks for flying Goosey airways and please hold tight, little Roger the Dodger!' 'Ok, captain. Let's get going! Goodbye, Lady Sig,' said Little Roger the Dodger. Lady Sig waved goodbye.

'We're clear and getting higher and higher,' Goosey said. 'Wow, this is cool. I have never been so high up. Let me reach for my goggles.'
'Hold on tight, Roger!'

'Whoa! I'm falling off, Goosey! You know, I don't have a flying license.'

Okay, okay. I got it. Let's do this. Golly Geese, it is so beautiful up here. I can see the whole city and the beautiful countryside,' Roger said

A butterfly landed on Roger's nose. 'Where did you come from and who are you? asked Roger.

Well, since you asked,' said the butterfly, 'Argentina is where I am come from and my name is Lady. I'm on my way to a meeting with the butterfly boss. I figured I would rest my wings if that's okay? It's been a tiring flight.' 'Of course, it's ok. Maybe we could drop you off somewhere?

'That would be great' said Lady.

'Is that where your boss lives? Is that her over there?'
Roger asked.

'Yes, that's her right there.'

'Hello, little Lady! How was your flight?

'It was good but tiring. The wind blew me here, there, and everywhere.

'Who are your friends?' The butterfly boss asked.

'Oh! This is Little Roger the Dodger and his friend Goosey.'

'Hello, butterfly boss, said Roger. 'This is Goosey
'Well, hello,' said the butterfly boss. 'My name is Bridget.
I'm not really a boss, I just make it my job to care for all
butterflies as they are so very important to our world's
ecology, 'Why are they so important?' asked Roger.

'There is a serious need for pollinators in the world and they should be protected.'

'Pollinator? What does that mean?'

'That's a great question, Little Roger. You see, every animal plays an important role in the cycle of life. The butterflies' role is to spread the pollen from plant to plant so they can flourish the world.

'Wow,' said Roger, 'I didn't know that but now I understand. Very sorry but we have to go now.'

'I hope to see you again,' said Bridget. 'Have a safe trip, Little Roger the Dodger and hold on tight to Goosey.

'It was a pleasure to meet you, Miss butterfly.

On a beautiful starry night, Roger asked Goosey: 'What is that ahead of us?' 'That used to be a big iceberg, Roger. It seems to be getting smaller and smaller every time I see it. It looks more like an ice cube now. And I know who lives there. That is if they are still there.'

'There they are! It's Walter and his family, the biggest walruses I've ever seen.
'Wave to them, Roger,' Goosey commanded and Roger shouted: 'Hey, there!'

'Hey Goosey, how's it going?' asked Walter, 'Who are you giving a ride?'

'This is little Roger the Dodger. I am giving him a ride home. He wants to check on his parents.

That's cool. Could you give me a ride to the new iceberg?

'No, I don't think so. You're a bit too heavy.' 'I know,' 'said Walter.

'I was just joking,' Goosey said, 'if I spot a place for you, I'll let you know!'

Got it,' said Walter.

'See you guys next time. Have a safe trip.'

'I think I'm flying first class on Goosey airways. I think I'm going to take a nap,' said Roger.

'ROGER, ROGER WAKE UP and hang on!' exclaimed Goosey all of a sudden.

'YIKES, cried Goosey 'My gosh, it's a JUMBO JET !!'

Goosey said: 'I hope it doesn't hit us.'

'That was close,' said Goosey. Goosey and Little Roger the Dodger started choking and spluttering. 'HukL,hukl,hukl...' said Goosey. coughing. 'It was all those exhaust fumes that came out of the Jumbo jet's engines.

'Goosey, can we stop and get something to eat?'
'Great idea, we could stop at the giant redwoods on the coast of California, especially since we have to cross the Pacific Ocean next.'

'Goosey, I don't know how to thank you enough for taking me all this way.'

'No need to thank me, Little Roger the Dodger. Helping others is the right thing to do.'

'Wow! That's a beautiful sunset and such a blue ocean, Goosey.'
'Yes, it is Little Roger the Dodger. We are headed south now.'

'Hey Roger,' said Goosey, 'can you see all the flying fish?'

'Yes. They can fly?'

'Yes, not quite as far as me but still, they are great flyers.'

'Goosey exclaimed Roger, 'I can see a big fish or a whale.'

'Oh, that is not a fish or a whale, Roger. It's a lot of plastic.'

'Plastic?' Asked Roger. 'Why is it in the ocean?'

'Some people just throw their waste in the ocean when really, they shouldn't.'

'That's not very good for all fish that live there.' Roger's voice sounded sad.

'Hey Roger, let's stop before our next flight.'
'That sounds great, Goosey. Which island is the one
with lots of palm trees and mountains?'
'It's Bora Bora.'

'The island is awesome. I am the king of this island,' declared Roger.

'You certainly are,' confirmed Goosey?

'I thought I was, who's is this?'

'Hey there, what's your name?' asked Roger.

'My name is Charles but just call me Charlie.'

'Sorry for jumping up and down on top of you Charlie,' Roger apologized.

'No problem, why are you guys in Bora Bora?'

'I'm on my way home to Kangaroo Island,' Roger explained.

'Ah, Australia, yes. I was there in 1939.'

'What!!? 1939? That was a long time ago. If I subtract 1939 from 2021 that would make you 82 years old.

'Yes, that's correct. I was born on this beech a long time ago.'

'Do you want to go for a swim?' Charlie suggested.

'I don't know how to...,' said Roger.

'Ok, how about skiing then?

'This is so cool. I wish I could swim like you. And by the way Charlie, please come visit me at home.'
'I sure will.'

'There is your mom's and dad's island, Roger,' Goosey announced.

'I hope they are safe in the green forest. I can see where the rest of the island was burned.'

Roger, hold on tight. We are going in for a landing, ready?'

'Ready,' answered Roger.

'HELLO. HELLO,' shouted Roger. 'Mom. Dad. Hello. It's me, Little Roger the Dodger.'

'HEY WROGER, COUSIN WROGER, I missed you!'
'Hey there, little guy.' Roger was really happy to
see him.

'Mom. Dad.' Roger was overexcited. 'Are you okay? I have been so worried about you. I'm so happy to see you. guys.'

'Hello Son,' said Dad. 'We are so grateful to be safe. And now you are here with us that just makes everything perfect,' Dad smiled Mom was so happy.

'My Little Roger the Dodger, I thought about you every day, I have missed you so much,' Mom cried out.

'Our part of the forest was unharmed but food was in very short supply. Therefore, we are replanting seeds to save the forests and have food for everyone,' explained Roger's mom.

'What can I do to help, mom?' Roger asked eagerly.

'Well, you are here now. That's a very important start. We all love you so much.

'London is a terrific city but getting home means everything to me. I escaped the zoo, rode an awesome bike, had a lady with a sparkly hat that waved at me riding down the river...' Roger told his mom and dad.

'A sparkly hat?' asked mom, wondering if she had heard correctly. What color was the car she was in?'

'Black,' Roger answered, surprised at the sudden interest. 'Was she sitting in the front of the car or in the back of the car?'

'She was in the back seat.'

'Well, Roger, that was the Queen of England.'

'WHAT? The Queen?? I had no idea it was the Queen. But I know what color she likes,' Roger said proudly.

'Well, Mr. Goosey, I cannot say how grateful we are that you brought my son home.'

'You are very welcome, Mrs. K,' said Goosey.

'Please, come back and visit again. You are always welcome, Mr. Goosey.'

'Thank you, I will,' said Goosey with a big smile.

'Bye Goosey, they all said.

'See you guys very soon. Take care of yourself, little Roger the Dodger!'

Dear Reader,

When Goosey said to take care of myself, I suddenly remembered officer Dibbs saying the very same thing to me. I think he purposely left my cage open so I could escape which was very kind of him. He also said: 'It's not how you start out, it's how you finish that counts.' Thinking about that, I know now how I'm going to start out. First - by helping my Mom and Dad replant the forest. And then, I will help everyone understand that the earth should be very important to us. During my flight home, I understood that officer Dibbs was right. It is the pollution that is making our planet hotter. I think I have a plan.

I am going to start the Little Roger the Dodger's reclamation club where I'm going to teach everyone how to plant, reuse, recycle and renew everything, to help stop the polluting of our planet. Ask your parents, and they can also tell you about the things you can do to help stop the pollution. And please visit;

www.littlerogerthedodger.com

So, think big. Dream big. Maybe one day your help can solve problems and help everybody. The world was made by dreamers. And you know, it matters not how much or how little you do, just doing something can make a difference. Thank you for reading my story. Yours truly, Little Roger the Dodger

www.ingramcontent.com/pod-product-compliance
Lightning Source LLC
Chambersburg PA
CBHW041540260326
41914CB00015B/1513